THE SELECTED LYRIC POETRY

of

MAKSYM RYLSKY

*Translated from Ukrainian
by Michael M. Naydan*

GLAGOSLAV
PUBLICATIONS

THE SELECTED LYRIC POETRY OF MAKSYM RYLSKY

by Maksym Rylsky

Translated by **Michael M. Naydan**

Publishers Maxim Hodak & Max Mendor

© 2017, Michael M. Naydan

© 2017, Glagoslav Publications

www.glagoslav.com

ISBN: 978-1-911414-41-4

This book is in copyright. No part of this publication may be reproduced, stored in a retrieval system or transmitted in any form or by any means without the prior permission in writing of the publisher, nor be otherwise circulated in any form of binding or cover other than that in which it is published without a similar condition, including this condition, being imposed on the subsequent purchaser.

THE SELECTED LYRIC POETRY

of

MAKSYM RYLSKY

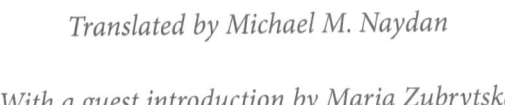

Translated by Michael M. Naydan

With a guest introduction by Maria Zubrytska

Maksym Rylsky

(1895–1964)

ACKNOWLEDGMENTS

My translations of Rylsky first appeared in a bilingual edition *Autumn Stars: Selected Poetry of Maksym Rylsky*, which was published by Litopys Publishers in 2008. My gratitude to Mykhailo Komarnytsky of Litopys for the care he gave in preparing that volume for publication. Many thanks also to the Lviv artist Jurij Koch for the imaginative cover he did for that bilingual edition. I am grateful to Maria Zubrytska for her thorough comparison of my translations to Rylsky's originals in early drafts of many of these translations. They are considerably improved as a result of her expertise. I also have a large debt of gratitude to Myroslava Prykhoda for taking the time to go over sticky problems in the final version of the first edition of the translations with me. This new edition contains a number of emendations from that earlier version. Any errors or omissions, of course, are mine.

This edition is dedicated to
Alex and Helen Woskob

Between the Lyric and Ideology: the Duality of Maksym Rylsky's Poetic World

*There is a poem by Verlaine
in which the poet asks himself
in bitter remorse: "What have you,
a reckless man, done with your life?"*

Maksym Rylsky

In the history of Ukrainian literature Maksym Rylsky's creative oeuvre comprises an illustrative example of political violence versus poetic talent, when under coercive circumstances the poet's vision of the world breaks up in two: into a lyrical perception of the world on one hand and into an ideological one on the other. The best proof of this dichotomy or split of the dimension of Maksym Rylsky's creative imagination may be the structural and semiotic cartography not solely of all his works, but of the titles of all his thirty-five collections of poetry published during his lifetime as well. The very number of his collections of poetry alone indicates a certain obsession with the ardent zeal of the poet to adhere to his principle of compensation or a symmetric balancing of coerced ideological involvement with the unconstrained vital force of the lyrical word no matter what. In this respect Maksym Rylsky is indeed the most paradoxical Ukrainian poet, whose answer to political violence was a lyric explosion, whose mission apparently was escape from his ultimate failure both as a Person and as a Poet.

The early poetry collections of Maksym Rylsky are characterized by a neo-romanticism that flows into Symbolist poetics, which captivated the poet under the influence of the French Symbolists Baudelaire, Rimbaud, Mallarme, and Verlaine as well as the Russian Symbolists Blok and Annensky. The poet supplemented his neo-romantic and Symbolist predilections with his fascination with folk songs as well as with his interest in the principles of musical organization of poetic texts. For this reason, his sonnets and octaves have the feel of songs. In his subsequent collections Maksym Rylsky prefers classical poetic forms: the tercet (terza rima), the octave and sonnet, and different metric feet from the hexameter and iamb to *vers libre* appear in his poetry. Owing to such a wide range of different styles and poetics in the texts of Maksym Rylsky, the Ukrainian word acquired a new resonance. Already in 1925 Mykola Zerov, one of the most interesting Ukrainian theoreticians of literature and Neoclassicist poets, underscored the dominance of the features of the Neoclassicist style in the poet's oeuvre of that time. In particular, Mykola Zerov emphasized the equilibrium and clarity of form, exceptional melodiousness, the combination of ingenuousness with elegance along with an aphoristic nature. This prominent literary theoretician underscores the refinement and at the same time sophistication of the architectonics of the poet's lyric texts, his natural simplicity in the creation of poetic images-reincarnations, including self-metamorphosis and self-transformation.[1] This observation is particularly important for the understanding of the radical self-metamorphoses in Maksym Rylsky's oeuvre under the ideological tension of the repressive Stalinist regime.

Maksym Rylsky as a lover of life, who observed the beauty of nature with enchanted eyes and who, with a pure and almost childlike rapture celebrated it in his poetic images, rich in associations and personifications, managed in his early poetic oeuvre to grant the status of event to the most prosaic of things, and to transform the most ordinary scene into an artistic poetic canvas that fascinates the eye and ear. The synthesis of his color palette, the phonetic melodiousness of polyphonic sound, and the ability to evoke tactile sensation in the reader comprise the most characteristic features of Maksym Rylsky's poetic masterpieces. His creative work is abundant with examples of this artistic synthesis; the motifs of the autumnal garden with ripe apples ("These apples ripened so prematurely," "The apples ripened, the apples are red") and the subtle poetization of the image of grapes and roses deserve particular attention. In Maksym Rylsky's poetic garden "real" becomes "abstract" and becomes elevated to the highest form of aesthetization and vice versa. The notion of beauty is always deeply rooted in the the hard work ethic involved in tending a garden well:

---

[1] Zerov, Mykola. *Literaturnyi shliakh Maksyma Ryl's'koho: Tvory v 2-kh tomakh*, II (Kyiv: Dnipro Publishers, 1990).

> He cherishes his little garden as he would cherish a child
> He talks to it with tenderness every day;
> He digs around and ties up raspberry branches,
> He cuts dead branches off cherry trees.

or the extended metaphorization of the image of language as a grapevine:

> Cherish your language,
> A you would cherish a sprout of the vine;
> Weed your garden
> Carefully and diligently.
> Let language be
> Purer than a tear…

Perhaps the poet consciously chooses this very poetization of the natural connection between the meaning of the Latin word "cultura" (to cultivate) and its modern meaning as a stage of human civilization established by the algorithms of human behavior and by the symbolic structures that make this behavior meaningful and significant. In the poet's artistic presentation this formula of transformation of the "culture" concept has a masterfully unsophisticated metaphorical articulation:

> Human happiness has two wings:
> Roses and grapes – both beautiful and useful

In this context we should underscore the polysemantic symbol of grapes with their rich variational component, which, in Maksym Rylsky's creative imagination, has the very significant connotation of "usefulness – sacrifice," which, at the same time, is characteristic of the poet's oeuvre. The frequent characterization of the symbolic image of grapes in the poet's creative oeuvre, the dynamics of its modification from one collection of poetry to another, gives us grounds to assume that this image occupies a very privileged place in the axes of Maksym Rylsky's poetic thinking. Beginning with his early collections of poetry, grape symbolism as well as the symbol of the rose or blooming garden is predominant in world baroque poetry in general and in Ukrainian poetry in particular; suffice to mention *The Garden of Divine Songs* by Skovoroda. Mykola Zerov was the first to comment on Rylsky's predilection for neobaroque forms, for its syntax and symbolism, along with the distinctive neoromantic and Symbolist aspirations of the poet: "first he will flow in the poetic lines with a capricious stream of the nearly colloquial syntax of Mickiewicz ('The Boat,') then he will take a motif of Franko and decore and debaroque the strict architectonics of its monumental masses beyond recognition") ("Wanderers").[2]

The cartography of Maksym Rylsky's poetry collections clearly demarcates the lines between exclusively lyric titles and ideologically engaged or conditionally neutral titles. Let us take for example the poet's early collections of poetry such as *On White Islands* (1910), *Under Autumn Stars* (1918), *The Blue Distance* (1922), *Poems* (1925), *Through a Storm and Snow* (1925), *The Thirteenth Spring* (1926), the titles of which reflect the neoromantic and Symbolist disposition and aspirations of the poet. Such poetry collections as

---

2   *Ibid.*, 561.

The Sound and Echo (1929) and *Where Roads Meet* (1929), which were called Maksym Rylsky's "poetic death" by Jurij Lavrinenko), can be considered the beginning of the transformation of the poet's conception of the world.[3]

By the way, the titles of these collections of poetry alone comprise a distinct marker of the motif of the harmony and possible union of two parallel worlds: the world of the creative imagination and the other not very appealing world of reality. This statement requires a brief contextual explanation. In the 1920s of the past century Rylsky was a member of the group of talented poets and literary critics that is known in the history of Ukrainian literature as the school of Ukrainian Neoclassicist writers. Besides Rylsky, the school is represented by Mykola Zerov, Mykhailo Drai-Khmara, Pavlo Fylypovych, and Osvald Burghardt (whose pen name was Yuri Klen). Neoclassicist writers considered themselves aesthetes with a distinctive predisposition for classical simplicity, exalted feelings, a deep insight into the philosophical essence of existence, and the refinement of poetic language and advanced excellence in poetic versification. Numerous ideological adversaries of Neoclassicist aesthetics accused its proponents of deliberate escape from reality, of a reluctance to celebrate the achievements of the Bolshevik Revolution and to reflect on the burning issues of post-revolutionary reality. Perhaps this is the reason why Maksym Rylsky responded to these straightforward and tactless accusations in his own way in "a chapter from the poem 'Sashko'" that contains evident ironic digressions

---

3 Lavrinenko, Jurij. *Liryka i lirychnyi epos Maksyma Ryl's'koho*, Vol. 2 (Kyiv: Ukrains'ke slovo, 1994): 94.

with a distinct critique of the political, socio-cultural and literary atmosphere in Ukraine at that time:

> I know every single world,
> And these worlds are sacred,
> But time after time we make them
> A sacrifice to our secret goal.

In the late 1920s clouds gathered over all those who had a clear-cut artistic, public and socio-political position, and who were not afraid to defend it openly. The ten-year period of rapid development of Ukrainian culture, literature and art that is known as the "Ukrainian Renaissance" became the subject of severe criticism by Stalin and his menials. Shortly thereafter staged trials took place, the scenario of which was accurately described by Franz Kafka in his novel *The Trial*. They were directed exclusively at the most prominent and talented representatives of the Ukrainian intellectual elite. Maksym Rylsky was the first of the Neoclassicist writers who became a victim of Stalinist repressions. On his birthday on March 19, 1931 he was arrested on the preposterous charge of "membership in a counter-revolutionary organization." The poet was behind bars until August 1931. He was forced to give testimony against himself every day or sometimes even twice a day. These kinds of "testimony" and "self-denunciations" under intense psychological and often physical pressure comprise a characteristic phenomenon of the Stalinist period and unequivocally would require separate interdisciplinary research. The records of the investigation of his case (case #272 from the KGB archives) were first published in the journal Kyiv (#2, 1996) sixty years after the fact. In August 1931 Maksym Rylsky was released from prison due to a lack of evidence on his purported "terrorist" activity. The "coercively-voluntary" poetic celebration of Party ideology and of the workers' achievements of the Soviet people along with the status of an official Soviet writer comprised the price Rylsky paid for this freedom. This price would not have been so dramatic if not for the fact that Maksym Rylsky was the only Neoclassicist writer who remained alive and who subordinated his muse to the dictatorship of the Party. The majority of his friends, particularly Rylsky's sworn spiritual brother Mykola Zerov from the Ukrainian school of Neoclassicist writers were repressed and died in Stalinist labor camps. The collection of poetry *The Sign of Libra* (1932), in which the poet definitively switches from the poetics of his prior texts to the emphatic glorification of the achievements of the Party, became the ultimate turning point and the final break from his prior texts. Such poetry collections as *Kyiv* (1935), *Summer* (1936), *Ukraine* (1938), and *Grape Harvest* (1940) illustrate the dramatic plummeting of the poet's lyric talent in the context of the most tragic events in the history of Ukraine: the inhuman manmade famine of 1933 and the Stalinist repressions that were aimed at the extirpation of the Ukrainian intellectual elite. During the most sorrowful days when an ideological plague was being spread all over Ukrainian towns and villages, inundating them with unbearable suffering and deadly terror, Maksym Rylsky wrote and published one collection of poetry after another as if in the frenzied rhythm of a "dance macabre." When the muse of the aristocrats of the Ukrainian spirit grew silent, the official Communist Party mouthpieces would "force rhyme." However disappointing that may have been,

Maksym Rylsky, one of the most talented Ukrainian poets of the twentieth century who, as a result of political circumstances, failed to realize his full potential as a Poet.

Despite his falling into the abysses of ideological traps, Rylsky continually strove to sublimate the deep lyricism of his view and perception of the world into lines of poetry. The poem-vision "Thirst" comprises a characteristic example of such resistance to circumstances. Although it is disreputably dedicated to the "25th anniversary of Soviet rule in our glorious Ukraine," it is, in fact, modern in its form, and it encloses the text with a manifold system of explicit and implicit meaning. Of course, the surface of the text contains an ideological outline that is thin as a veil along with a curt glorification of the Party and its leaders, but in its depth the text comprises an artistic audiovisual composition of three voices and three silhouettes amplified with the themes of a fairytale and a "dream – beyond the dream." Interestingly, ideological motifs alternate with lyric ones in these themes, and the latter often resonate with the bitter acknowledgement of a devastated garden and a desolate home.

> Oh, geese, young geese!
> Descend today to take them on your wings!
> The earthly children! But no! In vain! In vain!
> My garden is a wasteland, my home a prison!

One can observe the poet's ambivalence between ideological poetry reflecting on topical issues of the day and his lyric sketches and confessions in the collections of poetry published in the 1940s and 1950s, such as *For the Homeland* (1941), *A Word about My Mother* (1942), *Weapon of Light* (1942), *Thirst* (1943), *The Burning Bush* (1944), *The Journey Back to Youth* (1944), *The Chalice of Friendship* (1946), *Fidelity* (1947), *Under the Stars of the Kremlin* (1953), *On the Resurrected Land* (1956), and *Autumn in Holosiyiv* (1959). In addition to these collections of poetry, Maksym Rylsky published four books of lyro-epic long poems, a series of translations from Slavic and West European literatures and scholarly works on linguistics and literary criticism. Among the most famous of Rylsky's translations are *Pan Tadeusz* by Adam Mickiewicz, *Hernani* by Victor Hugo, *Cyrano De Bergerac* by Edmond Rostand, *The Maid of Orleans* by Voltaire, *King Lear* and *The Twelfth Night* by William Shakespeare, and *Eugene Onegin* by Aleksandr Pushkin. The Communist Party generously rewarded its official poet with lofty titles and state prizes. In 1943 he was elected an academician; in 1943 and 1950 he received the State Prize of the USSR; in 1944-1964 Rylsky served as the director of the Institute of Art, Folklore Studies and Ethnology of the National Academy of Sciences of Ukraine; and in 1960 he was awarded the Lenin Prize.

In contemporary Ukrainian literary criticism scholars do not show particular interest in the figure and creative oeuvre of Maksym Rylsky. There are several reasons for this. In the first place, it has been a matter of priority to fill in gaps in Ukrainian literary history with the rehabilitation of those poets who were annihilated by the brutal Stalinist ideology machine and whose works were obliterated completely from the consciousness of the reader in view of various taboos and prohibitions. The vivid memory of those thousands and thousands of Ukrainian intellectuals who died a martyr's death in Stalinist concentration camps may comprise another factor. With this in view, the ideological conformism of those who managed to survive cannot be forgotten; because of that they are considered antagonists of the victims of Stalinist repression. The poet, whom Ukrainian literature of the twentieth century had been anticipating, became the victim of self-transformation and self-metamorphosis. As the voice of damnation of his poem-vision "Thirst," Rylsky doomed himself to eternal duality. At least, in that split of his poetic soul, one of the voices not only did not sing out of tune, but it reached the heights of poetic brilliance. Let us listen closely to that voice and open the lyric texts of the poet despite prevailing literary fashion. The poetry of Maksym Rylsky is still awaiting its attentive reader whom the poet had been anticipating for a long time and whom he addressed ardently and desperately, almost on the verge of his soul's scream:

> Reader! Look more closely with what
> I comforted my song,
> And perhaps then you will hear something
> That is more than just sounds and words.
>
> You will hear in my song
> The echo of your own hopes...
> Reader! Take a look, give a smile:
> I am yours, I am not dead, I am alive!

—Maria Zubrytska, Ivan Franko Lviv National University
—Translated by Olha Tytarenko, University of Nebraska

TRANSLATOR'S INTRODUCTION

Two things struck me on my first visit to the Rylsky Museum at the edge of the luxuriant oak trees of the Holosiiv Forest in the southwestern part of the city of Kyiv — one obvious, the other a bit subtler. As I passed by a small lake with paddleboats to my right, I came up to a seemingly endless number of long platform-like, concrete steps, each about a meter long. This was the only encumbrance to reach his house-museum at the top of the hill. Even if you're in good physical condition, it's still quite a few huffs and puffs to reach that road at the top. Perhaps that is one reason why Rylsky chose to live there after his arrest in 1931 — the secret police may have felt that the near vertical walk was not worth the trouble. I have been told that during his arrest Rylsky was paraded for four hours along the city streets with his arms forcibly raised above his head, so that everyone could glimpse the famous poet—and thus be warned by his fate. After the public humiliation, Rylsky was, fortunately, released, only to live in fear for most of the rest of his days. Despite the constant psychological terror of impending arrest, while living in Holosiiv, he could enjoy the beautiful oak forest as well as a modicum of peace and security provided by the seemingly endless steps. What was his crime? He was a lyric poet who never wrote any political verse. That was more than enough to be an enemy of the state in Stalin's time, particularly given the fact that Rylsky was a great poet who happened to write in Ukrainian.

It has been revealed in now open NKVD-KGB archives that over half of the 1500 or so writers purged by Stalin in the 1920s and 1930s were Ukrainian. Rylsky somehow managed to survive while many others did not. Perhaps it was partly his fame, the exalted role that poets play in Ukrainian culture; perhaps it was his acquiescence to the state imposed literary doctrine of socialist realism in the 1930s. The second, and a quite telling feature for me in the Rylsky Museum is a small figurine on Rylsky's writing desk — three monkeys hearing, speaking and seeing no evil. This was Rylsky's obvious path to salvation in impossible times. But in following the advice of the figurines, one also pays a certain price: Rylsky's output of significant lyric verse plummeted except for a few long poems penned during the wartime period of relaxed censorship, and a handful of inspired lyrics toward the end of his life in the late 1950s and early 1960s.

It is particularly impressive when you take note of the fact that Rylsky mastered the art of poetry at the precocious age of fifteen with a fully developed and mature poetic voice. Rylsky is a master particularly of two genres — the intimate love lyric and nature poetry. He would often combine both elements of his art in a single verse with the same kind of emotional reverence for his beloved that he had for nature. Both love and nature poetry for him comprise a vehicle to express a heightened sense of awareness of being, a hyperconsciousness of the joy of existence reflected in the surrounding world. Rylsky is one of those poets who comprehends that nature can profoundly transform our inner world, and that we as human beings are codependent on it as a source of sustenance and inspiration. It is, simply, an integral part of our soul. Rylsky also has a third focus in his poetry that serves as a steady source of support for him — the literary tradition and its thoughtful contributions to the development of civilization. In his poetry in the Neoclassicist tradition you will find embedded as well as open references (epigraphs, dedications, and poems) to Homer, Sappho, Dante, Lamartine, Annensky, Nietsche, Heine, Shakespeare, Baudelaire, and many others. For him the present can not be the present without the past. You will also observe a great reverence for contemporaries of Rylsky in his poetry, particularly for Mykola Zerov and Pavlo Tychna. Another of Rylsky's other long-abiding interests – native Ukrainian folklore and songs – can be found in the long poem "Thirst," which combines elements of the lyric with the epic in the poet's entreaty to save his homeland from destruction during World War II.

Rylsky was truly a Parnassian poet of extraordinary talent who was born as a poet and not made. This collection hopefully provides a representative selection of the best that his poetry has to offer.

> – Michael M. Naydan
> *Woskob Family Professor*
> *of Ukrainian Studies*
> *The Pennsylvania State*
> *University*

ON WHITE
ISLANDS
(1910)

A SLEEPLESS NIGHT

It's stifling, quiet and dark everywhere,
The darkness strangles me, an evil darkness,
The bright world is gone... Where are you, people,
Where have you disappeared? You're gone, all gone...

Threatening walls stand in silence,
Apparitions twist in a wild dance...
Where are you, beautiul one, where are you, happy one,
In the glow of beauty as if in an elegant wreath?

It's stifling... Open a window? No — quietly
Azure dreams fly into the window,
There's no place in the heart for them...
My heart broods and cries.

It's stifling and quiet... Where are you,
Enchanted dreams? Let one fly to me just for a moment!
Soulless walls, mute walls —
Move apart! And set me free!

***

As the pink evening descends onto the earth
I step out alone into a grove,
I'll look as the sun half asleep turns
The entire weary, worn-out land to gold.

Leaves will whisper a wondrous fairy tale,
One that is heard from the clouds,
And dreams will take wing over bright stars
To a far-off land of enchantments.

On silken wings, a bright sky-blue,
I'll rise up with them and fly off.
And once again in my thoughts there will be
No agony, no suffering, no weeping…

ON WHITE ISLANDS

I

The ocean immeasurably heavenly blue
    Spread high above the earth,
With cloud islands floating in this ocean.

Floating white islands as though made of snow —
    I fly at you... at least in my thoughts,
So that you can shelter my heart with serenity's charms.

II

White, buoyant somnambulant clouds
    Float quietly;
Tenderly peaceful and melodious everywhere
    They pour out their charms.

III

I float along on a cloud island
    In the heavens,
No longer living on earth!

Around me a ray of light gleams
    And, like a bird,
The cloud flies into the far-off unknown.

IV

Farewell, suffering
    And the agony of love!

Farewell, entire earth, unwashed by tears,
Where in grief, alone, I grew up sorrowful...
    Now I'm in space,
    In an azure sea!
Here the sun is brilliant,
Lovingly powerful
It still stitches a bright golden headscarf...
Carefree, peaceful, I'll quietly fall asleep
    Beneath a sweet ray of light
    On a white island...

V

I awakened... the wind is blowing,
Gathering black clouds into a cluster,
Tearing apart the white ones...
A frightened sun no longer warms...

Black clouds tore out
The tender, golden threads...
All the snowy white islands
Began to tremble from fear.

Lightning plays in a cloud,
Thunder rumbles in threatening anger...
Timid white clouds,
Where have your charms gone?

.   .   .   .   .   .

Rain falls from the sky in streams,
There is mighty power in those streams,
The thirsty earth drinks them up
And giggles like a little girl...

VI

Once again the sun stitches a golden headscarf,
      A rainbow plays in the azure,
And there, below, pure silver droplets
      Glitter on the trees and grass.

Once again the sun stitches a golden headscarf,
      And the floating white islands
Once again pour out their light and carefree charms,
And the heart beats in joy.

VII

The evening rushes about,
The somnambulant evening,
The sun hides from view.
      The evening rushes about,
      Harmonius song somewhere
      Pours out.
The evening rushes about...
The nightingale's song is
There, on the earth.
      The evening rushes about...
      The peaceful island
      Disappears in the fog.

VII

I sleep and dream... On a floating island,
In azure, silver and golden attire
In indescribable beauty Fairies are walking and glowing.

In their braids the stars play like gems,
Like enchanted heavenly flowers,
And all of them so amiably nod their heads.

And a handsome young man steps out of the forest,
And the moon shines on his high forehead...
I sleep and dream on a floating island.

IX

The sun rises, the sun plays,
Pouring out smiles every which way,
It scatters graces, and it sows them
Through the darkness — and warms,
Chasing away the darkness of night...
> There below are choirs of birds,
> There in luxurient attire Floras,
> Trees stand and laugh...
> Singing pours out... and tears too...
> Ah! Grief has stirred there!

X

On a floating island
> I've forgotten about grief,
I'm happy in the mighty
Azure sea.

XI

These are just daydreams, only daydreams...
> Yes... I'm on the earth,
Where at least the sun shines and warms,
> And the whole world is in a fog...

.   .   .   .

Daydreams, daydreams, so golden,
> Why are you just daydreams,
Fiery impulses of the heart,
> Why are you... without hope?..

BENEATH THE AUTUMN STARS, I
(1918)

***

I wait for a word from you,
But I am as silent as night,
In the rustling of an oak grove
I hear the clamor of sobbing.

I lean over in expectation,
But you are as silent as the day
That in summer has grown weary
From happiness and songs.

***

These apples have ripened so prematurely,
And prematurely there is silence in the heart,
The straight birches have turned gold
      And summer is passing.

Recently the nightingales in a flowering valley
Were laughing clammily, praising love…
There is no more recent past. And that which is today —
      Will it come again?

THE LAST

Quieter... Stand there. Don't speak.
Let's say good-bye for the last time.
Can you see? The campfire on the mountain
Is flickering out in quiet agony.

Everything has ended, the night has passed —
We never even dreamt of happiness...
What, it's morning already? You've gone?
Everything is over, all over.

You left like a pale shadow,
The shadow of unrealized fate...
Who, you dope, would sob over something
That gave you only pain?

***

Who painted broad-leafed chestnut trees
    On a background of blue?
Who dressed the bosom of the earth
    In tenderly beaming colors?

Who gave me my full-voiced spirit?
    And the joy of youthful days?..
Who created these tears
    And the gem-like dew?

***

In solitude I leaf through
Pages of our conversation,
And on my forehead I still sense
                The warmth of your hand.

Motionless shadows. Gray walls.
A candle blinks uncertainly.
The sleepless night flows slowly
                And remains silent.

The white candle has already burned out —
And soon it will burn out in my heart...
You're not here. You flew away
                Like an instant.

***

Il n'est rien de commun entre la terre et moi.[4]

A. de Lamartine

Ridiculed by myself
Fooled by foolish life,
I am walking with pain and sorrow,
And inexpressible remorse.

I am looking for a white lily —
But all the lilies are in mud!
I am looking for my land,
But this land — is foreign to me…

---

4   There is nothing in common between the earth and me.

***

I don't know whether it's love or not…
Shadow, sorrow, silence,
There's no life anywhere,
In the world you are — alone.

It happened once — or was it a dream…
Forgotten — or passed…
In my soul human good and evil
Were destroyed long ago.

In darkness branches grow gray.
No movement or people…
There is just one thing in this world.
The fire of your eyes.

***

Lights. A rowdy evening.
An alluring veil…
And the deceptively bright distance
Of the city's sky.

And that deep voice,
And the light tap of her feet,
And in the heart is the hushed moan
Of incomprehensible torments.

THE VOICE OF POISON

I love the poison hidden in the lily,
I love a flaw exposed in the open,
And the brazenness of your tenderness,
And the unfamiliar smoke of harsh caresses.

I love you because you are foreign to love.
For you alone have remained for me;
I love in you my last love,
The sweet froth of quaffed wine.

A WINTRY PANE

So sad, so boundlessly sad.
All is over. (Did it happen?)
I gaze fixed and emptied of thoughts
Through winter's frosty pane.

On this clear night everything is lucid,
But there is no farther to go:
Life is joyful and sweet,
But not for those without a purpose…

TO MY LEONORA
A Drunken Sonnet

No, you are not here, not in the world.
You appeared in the autumn night,
And I met your lips, partly open,
Devoutly like a sacred relic.

You appeared quietly to awaken me.
To flash and then dissolve in shadow.
To forever leave a recollection in my heart
Of that sweet night, so clear and deep blue.

The pure images of women float past.
In them I seek — a reflection — yours …
Those very lips and unfathomable sparkling eyes.

But something is missing. Why? I don't know.
Eternal pain and agony rock my heart…
No, you are not in the world, woman with white hands.

***

Like a kiss through a veil —
Wondrous, endless and tender —
In the heart an old regret has arisen
And has disappeared like a gust of wind.

Your face and your voice
That at the moment of parting beckons and calls;
A sudden fiery gaze
And suddenly secret contempt.

All passed before me at that moment
Like a bolt of lightning…
But a lightning bolt cannot ignite
The placid lake in your heart!

***

Shadows are shifting along the valley,
  A pond is dozing.
You can barely see the cobalt blue
  And boundless sky.

There far away stars are shifting
  In the expanses,
Like seagulls in a blue sea,
  In a sea so blue.

They're shifting in eternal solitude
  And with sorrow,
Like shadows along the valley
  Beneath me.

***

The café is empty. The minions are murmuring,
Getting bored stiff without any boring work.
I'm sitting alone; my heart is remembering
Something distant as though I were drowsy.

A blurred twilight spreads through the room,
Though it's daytime outside the walls. It was just
Yesterday that the lips of my love chirped
To me of happiness, of tall mountains,

Of the dawn, of joyful anticipation,
Of the clinking of glasses and pure repartee…
To me it seemed: even of love,
Of the first blossom of not your first love…

It passed, and in your heart comes alive,
Like a lily in evening gold…
In the café the minions are murmuring quietly,
In the café it's a time of sweet drowsiness.

***

In a deep remote spot,
Far away from people,
Sleepy lilies bloom,
And it's quiet around the lilies.

In a deep remote spot
The green tone of water,
And red reflections
Fall onto the remote spot.

Here there are fetters and rules
And the hustle and bustle are awful…
But in the clear remote spot there is
Translucence, silence.

***

How sweet it is in midnight silence
To leaf through books you read long ago.
And again – with joy and sadness – to come across
Everything that you dreamt in a half-forgotten dream.

Back then spring beat its wing along your heart,
And age-old music intertwines and falls,
And what seems to have been a half-forgotten dream
Flashes in the haze as a new ray of light.

***

Love nature not like a symbol
    Of your soul,
Love nature not for your own sake,
    Love her for her own.

She's not only the subject of a poem
    Or a painting,
In her there are immeasurable heights
    And sacred depths.

She has a mighty soul,
    She has passion
That's greater than the entire passion
    Of your soul.

She is a mother. Be then her son
    And not an aesthete,
Then you'll become a living poet
    And not just a paper one!

BENEATH THE AUTUMN STARS, II (1926)

***

Dew has settled onto the white buckwheat,
Cheerful bees have begun to buzz,
The hundred-voiced field has grown silent,
In the embraces of a golden mist.

The road winds through the fields…
You will not come on foot or fly —
In my heart you will only chime
With faraway songs.

***

Summer stopped on the doorstep
And breathes a flame on everything,
And the weary wind carries
The threats of proud thunder.

Green summer is washing itself
And will laugh like a child —
Will I see the return
Of spring and spring flowers?

Will my spring dreams come true?
Will the summer not betray them?
Will it not scatter them
Like down on golden willows?

1911-1918

***

Snow fell silently and evenly
Fires smokily died down,
And a distant bell stood so strangely
In incomprehensible silence.

The two of us walked without speaking,
You were all covered with snow,
Snowflakes played and glimmered like stars
Above the sorrow of your silent forehead.

And people vaguely floated past,
They disappeared and faded like a dream —
And we walked aimlessly
In the snowy evening silence.

1911-1918

***

For Ivan Rylsky[5]

In the spring we used to ride to the field
On an old one-horse cart.
The corn sprouts turned slowly,
The groves turned green like smoke.

Rising above the silver of the
Forest's water, a tiny goldfinch chirped…
We rode together in silence
Knowing boundless happiness.

Work was frenzied in the field,
Oxen grew gray on the tillage.
In the evening a quiet drowsiness
Silently floated along the land.

Blissful we rode home
In the fresh evening haze,
And weary souls merged
With the living soul of the land.

---

5 The poet's older brother (1880-1933).

***

The field blackens... Clouds pass.
They embroider the sky in whimsical play.
The azure flocks of the first snowdrops...
Earth! How warm it is for us to be with you.

The distance deepens. The river turns blue.
The river turns blue, yawns and laughs...
Where do I put you, my green hopes?
There are so many of you that my heart will burst!

1911-1918

***

The lilacs are blooming, the orchard turning white
And quietly losing its petals,
Half-forgotten it dreams again
Like the wave of a precious hand.

In the sky the curly-haired wind
Rocks the warm azure,
And sways the grass on the earth,
And quiets down, then stirs up again,

Then suddenly on its wings it clutches
The undulating songs of cranes —
And an age-old fairy tale, eternally charming,
Pours out through the undulating song.

***

Like Odysseus, wearied by wandering
Over the deep blue sea. I — wearied by life —
Lay down beneath the shadow of an old black poplar,
I buried myself in its leaves and forgot everything.

Certain thoughts — or their shadows — scurry
In quiet drowsiness. A leaf gleams,
The white reflection of the sun falls on a trunk.
And a tiny bug crawls along it.

And I will fall asleep to the carefree rustling
With the hope that playing with a ball,
Tender Nausicaa[6] will awaken me,
The slender daughter of the Phaecian king.

---

6   The beautiful Phaeacian princess who discovers Odysseus at Scheria while she is washing clothes on the shore.

***

The apples ripened, the apples are red!
You and I are walking in the orchard along a path,
You, my love, will lead me to a field,
I'll go my way — and maybe come no more.

Love has already ripened under the warm rays,
And joyful lips have torn it off —
But now in my heart something is quivering and playing,
The way a golden branch quivers in the sun.

Hey, the fields are turning yellow, and the sky turning blue,
The plowman barely looms in the field…
Kiss me for the last time, hold me for the last time;
Only one able to love knows how to part.

1917

***

The rain has ended. The azure is clearing.
Will you come? Or fly to me?
Or will you reverberate with the fresh breath
Of hope like big drops of rain?

Or will you leave the azure of clear and
Fair days in my dark heart?
Birds fly above the earth along their way.
The rain has stopped reverberating.

***

There is a name, a woman's, soft and clear;
In it there is love, and sorrow, and hope;
Like a spring sigh it resounds:
    Maria.

Like the fragrance of the violet in spring mist,
Like a girl's song in snow and drifts,
Like a star it shines above the sadness of the earth:
    Maria.

Let me douse the hallowed in my heart,
Let me fall in empty battle —
And the last word I will write is:
    Maria.

BLACK ROSES

We were walking in a strange city
In murky indigo darkness.
We didn't feel like going home,
And weren't drawn to the earth.

We were walking in a crowd. Trembling people
Lit up, then grew dim in the silence.
I pinned black, otherworldly roses
Onto the bodice of your dress.

Silent carriages sailed along
In the clear golden chill.
"Where are you sailing, joyful people?"
Your silken voice asked.

And we stopped by a lake.
Silence gripped us.
All sounds drowned in the lake.
The moon swirled like smoke.

And I heard nothing else,
Though you said something to me.
And I tossed the black, otherworldly
Roses at your feet.

MUSIC

To the memory of Innokenty Annensky[7]

In the night they swooped down —
A black whirlwind in the black world —
Both daughters and sons began to lament
That their parents, their parents had been killed.

Wait a bit! it will not pass you,
It will not take pity on bright-faced infants:
It will crucify you on a tall cross
And scatter you over a wide field...

Who is this playing a dance for death,
Bobbing his head in time to it?
How her royal crown
Beams like jeweled ice!

A black whirlwind, the terror of the unknown,
Unattained, broken sacred relics...[8]
...With a spectral bow in the hands
Of Pagannini's Florentine nights.

1918

---

[7] Russian translator and poet (1855-1909), who greatly influenced both the Russian Symbolists and Acmeists (Anna Akhmatova, Nikolai Gumilev and Osip Mandelstam).

[8] Relics here could also be translated as shrines or temples.

***

Outside the walls the cold night is blowing;
A fire goes out, then begins to glow again…
Ah, it's been so long since I've heard human voices,
That I've already forgotten the simple language of the earth.

Do you know what? There, among people,
The very same mystery invisibly shines.
But they aren't able to see it in the darkness
With their feeble eyes.

***

It is not the clear-eyed image of Beatrice
And not the dark drunken look of a Bacchante[9]
That troubles me and ceaselessly calls
To the unknown distance, to the golden expanse.

No! a simple tiny face in a white kerchief,
Thin arms, the gold of long lashes
And a voice, somewhat childlike and timid,
Passed as a shadow in my soul.

...And the first night — the night first and last —
And the first word, the greatest of words,
That I first heard and first understood
In the garden in the whispering wind.

---

[9] One of the priestesses of Bacchus.

***

Frost! You are the s o u l o f a P a r n a s s i a n s i n g e r.
Just like she you hid in crystal,
the breath of waters, and the sorrows of stilled grass,
all from which hearts change.

And who can guess beyond the calm of lines
And the immaculate tones of blue
The deep singing of vernal floods
or summer storms and autumnal despair?

1919

***

For Bohdan Rylsky[10]

From your voice it's fragrant and wafts
With the sweet scent of cherry trees
That blossomed in clear hope
On a blue-eyed summer day.

The night, the moon, the willows, the rustling,
The hugs of arms and the joy of torments,
And the ardent nightingale's song
In ineffable blazing.

Over the surface of the pond sleepy grass,
Sweet sedge, the cry of lilies —
And the sweet and playful voice
Of children half in love.

---

[10] The poet's younger brother (1930-1991).

***

When everything in life's haze
Is lost and leaves no traces,
You don't want to go from or to home,
Because even there the fire has burned out long ago —

In you, art, in you alone there is
Shelter: in the beauty of unknown words,
In music that embodies beauty known to all
Into a heavenly play of colors.

In you, art, in a small painting
That is greater than the whole boundless world!
To you, art, and in your realm
I send you my1 respects and my warm greeting.

Your deeds — alone are everlasting,
And you among flowers are the brightest one.

***

Green shadows flashed along your soul —
The freshly-pure tone of soft moss,
The backwater of deep lightheartedness,
The past is reflected in what comes.

Be blessed, ears, that have heard
The golden law of sacred happiness!
It — in a wreath made of bunches of grapes —
Hasn't passed me by in a dirty tavern.

It came — it shone… The gently-blowing gift
Of boundlessness and unconstrained deep breath
Among life's dead phantoms!

A cold wind at dawn,
And the goldenness of the day grows in the east…
Be blessed, silent lips!

***

Eternity writes its unfinished folio
With a fiery quill,
And with tenderness wind sways
Petals of pensive roses.

Beauty walks, embroidering
Clear, deep skies in gold —
And with mud we trample
All that is beauty in us.

***

Let the cold, web-footed snow fall,
It will cover the field and fall on the glade,
Let it fill the paths around the house
And bring white silence into the house!

Friends and foes are rowdy around us,
Both family and strangers come pry into your soul —
And I in my incomprehensible sadness
Go from them all to the other side of the boundary.

Let the cold, web-footed snow fall,
Blocking the path from your friends and foes.
Let it cover the paths around the house,
Let it give me a chance to fall sleep

***

The tomatoes are already turning red
And autumn is striding along the grass.
What in blazes kind of sadness can there be
When our hearts are alive?

Tall asters, blue sky,
Your gaze, sweet and bright…
This all happened in a certain land,
I just don't know in which one.

So what if the end comes to
Autumn's charms? But right at that moment
A field of melons turns gold above the ravine,
As though a roofless lean-to is sleeping.

A tree bends from the weight of its fruit,
And, not terrifying for us, my child,
Is the time for the last trek
With no return — with no going back.

THE BLUE DISTANCE
(1922)

THE BLUE DISTANCE

I

In the world there is the singing Languedoc,
Joyful France blooms in Champagne,
Where in the sun each small town fades away
And villages wallow in grapevines.

Somewhere there is Marseille and a drunken spirit from the sea;
Somewhere there is Paris, the spirit of genius and waifs;
Somewhere Daudet[11] used to live, hot and bright;
Somewhere the pleasant Tartarins[12] used to hunt.

Somewhere there is an island that Shakespeare illumined
And where Dickens laughed through the fog,
And somewhere in Siberia a wild animal howls,
And caravans lope along the Sahara.

O my world! O distant laughter of girls
Who tear off sweet bunches of grapes!
May the grapes be blessed,
The autumn fruit of spring intoxication!

II

Let the Venetian waters at least in dreams,
The marble of steps and columns,
The glow of beauty and distant years,
And the gold of Madonnas be sorrowful.

---

11   French novelist Alphonse Daudet (1840-1897).

12   *Tartarin of Tarascon* is an 1872 novel by Alphonse Daudet.

Desdemona clothed in white
Stands on the steps above —
And above her brow is her crown
Made of the evening star's roses.

The watery road splashes,
Striking back golden fires,
And the doves of St. Mark
Have fallen asleep in blue silence.

You stretched out your arms, lily,
And a black warrior flew out
That in the white dreams of your soul
Darted out in a fire forever!

....

Let the distant journeys at least in dreams
Be without futile barriers —
And the joyfully sorrowful eyes
of Desdemonas in white!

III

Old tracery buildings
And each stone is the eternal trace
Of a long past love,
Of years that have died, of years eternal.

Coffee shops and towers, dreams with reality,
Rabelais and Rimbaud, flowers and grass,
And someone with a wonderful smile
Invites you into the unknown.

Violets, the ghosts of Versailles
And the carmine of lips, a drunken wedding,
And the acerbities of a strange ball
Through the poison of violins and the sorrow of trumpets.

You drank up the homebrew from a flagon
And are sleeping in filth next to the vat,
And somewhere there are pigeons, garrets,
Poets, the sun, and Paris!

1920

SILENCE
A Rondo

At a loss for words! An evening wind
Wafted above the fields. The bay glimmers
With far-off ships just like dreams...
                At a loss for words.

Who will verbalize the gust of the heavenly,
The sacred moment of creation in a frenzy
When the soul emerges from the shores?

But must you really put it into words,
Or , perhaps, will even song be sinful
At the time, when neither in us nor over us,
                We are at a loss for words?

1919

***

In the mountains among the stone and snows
Where the eye rarely sees the trace of a human,
A hunter's tiny hut, a haven for eagles,
Is distinctly painted on the azure sky.

A snowy muslin will cover the cliffs,
The Lord's wrath will grumble in the abysses —
We sit there, watching our kabobs on the spit,
We play chess and drink slowly.

Once as the pround Byron wrote
Manfred took rest in a hut just like this
To rise up against fate again.

So we — when the young day blooms —
We will go to play chess with death,
Stepping along the stony path.

1922

SONNET OF BOREDOM AND HOPE

There is nothing worse than being bored:
Not the bitterness of poison — the sourness of a lemon,
Nor the ranges in a fiery orchestra,
But the false mournful strum of a mandolin.

The fire passed and smoke was left,
The recollection of a storm — yellow creases of foam,
Caustic mist, where there once were a flood and thunder,
Where a spring flood-tide played — the croaking of frogs.

Even if there were only the criminal pride of a brow,
Even if Carmen should playfully pass
And drunken castinets should begin to clatter!

Even if there were some goblets, or a number of vices,
Even if there were poison in a golden ring,
Even if there were the strike of a cheerful stiletto!

1920

THE PHANTASMAGORIC BRIG
Octaves

I

I've forgotten you. Forgive me. Blue snow
Has drifted over my heart and window.
I float in daydreams on a phantasmagoric brig —
It's wide open, fresh, clear, and cold!
The last salutation to books and fetters,
And all is forgotten, as if it happened long ago,
It's as though it had dissolved, like evening gold,
In the silence of the last sorrow.

II

Tall masts, white sails
And damp wind, fresh and blustering.
Carry me, ship, carry me on!
Whoever streams to the distance is strong and happy,
In a land of variable beauty
One will lose unhealthy agonies and impulses,
Like Heine at the peak of good mountains...
Carry me — at least into a deadly vortex.

III

The helmsman is wise, the captain chipper,
The sailors not the kind to swig down a bottle.
God himself shows us the wide road
And reflects the path ahead with stars!
The Frenchmen are somewhere, the Karelians too,
And everyone eats, loves, and lives —

And somewhere bold lieutenants Hlan,[13]
Forgetting their loves, lather up the ocean.

IV

O joy of unseen shores!
I bow to you, my loftiestest gentlewoman!
Did I really live there in the house
When I mumbled something about my love,
When I captured moments of joy
For the earnest payment of eternal throes of death,
For human filth, for the whispers of friends,
And for the enmity of sisters and brothers?

V

Like Childe Harold courageously abandoning his
Homeland, which long ago had become foreign to him,
There I abandoned infinitely little,
And, it seems, I don't miss much of anything.
Some lone soul, I recall, was sobbing,
When finally I crossed the boundary;
And I must remind You, my love:
It wasn't You sobbing, but my mother.

VI

"My name is John, I'm a cook from a family of cooks.
Born in the Pacific Ocean.
A former cannibal baptized me.
To tell the truth I don't know who my parents were,
And that's why I learned to love the sea:

---

13   The hero of Norwegian novelist Knut Hamsun's (1859-1952) novel *Pan* (1894).

It's father, mother, and nursemaid for me.
Tell me, who are you, young foreigner?"
"I still haven't lived yet, but today I'm your brother."

VII

A storm approaches, howling and whistling,
Someone's chasing the clouds with a steel whip,
But we are bold, and we'll find a new bonfire
On a new shore,
With song and bottles we'll carry off
The entire past all the way to the new cemetery.
And we'll send our final letter home
In a bottle of burning rum.

VIII

Farewell, gentlewoman! The bottle has floated off!
The fresh wind toussles our hair
Above the frowns of a victorious brow!
All in a dream, distant, passed,
And covering everything an underwater haze,
in which gray-maned waves bluster.
Farewell, madam! You'll have to wait a while
For someone to manage to kiss You this way.

Winter 1920

***

A veranda, grapes, the humming of bees in white.
Glasses on a tablecloth. Tea the color of amber
Slightly steaming. Songs are somewhere, like waves,
And waves like songs. Each year spring is new!

Aphrodite emerges each year from the white foam,
And tritons and cupids splash around her,
And each time the mystery remains unrevealed,
And immutable laws have new content.

Every year cranes are in brightwinged harmony,
Every year there is the laughter of women and a weary rose —
And these are new lines in a white folio,
As though a dream for hearts, grown mute from happiness,
Green grapes and a golden veranda.

1921

***

Once again the road and splashes under the wheels
In the colors of chocolate and cinnamon,
And the forest is ready to fly off into the distance,
And the sound of an enchanted bell.

A lilac-colored alder is as close to me as a sister,
I don't have a sister. And my brothers have become estranged.
Like a hot candle the evening is burning out…
There's so little to live till night for us… so little.

1921

***

An unknown guest
Walks through blue fields,
Planting flowers of languor
Above us in rows.

The flame of the distant sun
Plays along our house,
And the unknown guest
Glimpses into our windows.

1918

***

Tristan saddles his horse
And rides off into a distant path.
Cawing flocks of ravens
Are carrying bad tidings.

Someone breaks his bow,
Another his helmet…
White-armed Isolde
Sobs at the window.

But the soul, like a bird,
Has fallen in love with the azure,
And dreams a new dream,
And the sky shimmers in gold —
Turning the lance into the same color.

1921

***

Once again I am riding on a wood-slat cart
With a merry bunch.
Willows bend over the water,
A bat flies up into the air.

Let recollections pour out after the wind
Like blue petals!..
My neighbor with a sly look
Is holding some long fishing rods.

Become a fisherman or a bird
If you want to forget about unwelcome tears!
Once again I'm riding on a wood-slat cart
And don't even want to look for happiness.

1919

SAPPHO TO APHRODITE
To M. Zerov[14]

Don't plait a golden net
For me,
You who were born
Of the foam of the sea.

Goddess, do not awaken
A young heart
During dark nights
In a stuffy bed!

Doves circle
Like white snowflakes,
Nightingales laugh
In a sacred grove.

Each one of them is your envoy,
A winged emissary…
For me the entire world —
Is a golden net.

1918

---

14   Mykola Zerov (1890-1937), poet, translator, and literary critic, who was one of the leaders of the Ukrainian Neoclassicist movement, which incuded Rylsky and several other poets in the 1920s.

NIETSCHE

In the high mountains he blessed
A serpent, man, the sun, and eagle:
Wisdom, light, the heart, the strength of wing —
For the sake of storms, happiness, and translucent heights.

The snake wrapped his brow
In madness; man unnoticeably conveyed
Thorns of thick thoughts;
The eagle had fallen to the earth, into decay and dust.

And he lifted his hands to the sun,
But it laughed treacherously —
And he fixed silence on his lips.

Alien to love and distant from wrath,
He descended along mysterious steps
Where wrath is dead and love not alive.

1922

HEINE

Harlequin with a rose in his hand
Walks amid the noisy carnival.
Cheeks and brow in farcical agony,
And in his eyes a distant reflection of grief.

Is it true, it's ridiculous to have faith and love,
Is it true, it's ridiculous to delight in flowers?
For how many years, how many centuries
People have known how to and kiss!

He laughs, so as not to sob,
He bounds to the sounds of a sarabande —
Yet Harlequin would be incapable
Of giving anyone a bloody rose!

1920

SHAKESPEARE

I wandered alone dressed as a poacher
In the green groves of England old,
And surrounding me in the foggy distance,
Jesters and kings came to me.

Sitting down on a stump in the middle of a glade,
I gazed at a misty spectacle,
And sketched the fine lines in it,
Giving eternity to the people in the fleeting.

The actor, a drunkard, a dreamer, and haughty,
I loved the insuperable downpours of words.
Love, agonies, jealousies, and anger,
The characters made of steel and silk.

1920

BAUDELAIRE

In a paradise of blissful torments where on thin stalks
The chimerical flowers of evil grow and coil.
Resembling the eyes of women and beasts,
His soul lived in a hellish paradise.

To frighten a bourgeois, to be called a cannibal
Who craved to eat the tiniest children;
To get drunk on the lonely, bitter, delicate mead
Of unfulfilled desires and dead ideas,

And to see in the wine of a shameless tavern
The wine of Communion, the very blood of Christ...
Is such a life, monstrous and chimerical,
                     Not called: Beauty?

1920

***

Fragrant roses adorned our wedding bed,
> The image of Cythereia[15] blesses it from the corner.

We will bring the goddess honey-sweet figs,
> Dark, strong wine and young doves.

The sun conceals itself in the sea, the roses
>> smell more intoxicating.
> Hands will seek hands, desirous lips – lips...

Give us the strength, goddess, to be beautiful in love
> And during a bewitching night conceive a wise son.

1921

---

15 Another name for Aphrodite. Cythera is an island off the southern coast of Peloponnesus known primarily as a center for the cult of Aphrodite.

***

In the warm days of grape harvesting
He met her. On slow moving mules
She returned from her bright garden,
As bright as a garden, and as joyful as laughter.

And he asked: "And how can I entice you
To turn you back to my arms?"
She said to him: "Light a lamp
To good Cythereia every day." She lifted the whip.

She shouted crisply and cheerfully at the mules,
And the right mule laid back its ear comically,
And dust flew up like pink smoke.

And he stretched like a child, and happily
Said: "It's good to be young
In the warm days of grape harvesting.

1922

THE THIRTEENTH SPRING (1926)

***

In thickets where you find only the paths of animals,
Among the monstrously intertwined branches,
A gentle blue clearing appears in the sky
Like a genial eye. Through a mysterious twilight,

The humming of pines, like the howling of the Furies,
The scratching of a lynx's claws, the hammer
Of an old woodpecker. For a weary man
It's so nice to reach a quiet spot,

The translucent look of cherished peace,
Where at times through the changing throng
The silver-woven smoke of tiny clouds will pass.

Thus you, art, amid the storms and twilight
Shine for people's thoughts and hearts —
A beaming eye in a dark sea.

***

The hoofprints have been covered in gray smoke,
A branch fell — a snowy paw,
And the wind, illusive and unseen,
Sways the dead trees.

And shadows pass to the sound of creaking
Of old aspens in icy bark,
And yet life appears to be just a shadow,
Suddenly a swarm of sparks flies in.

Then the train gushes with a screech and whistle,
Flashing its red eye on the snow…
Whom did you believe? The golden sparks
Or the gray hair of the hollow aspens?

1924

***

To circle in the golden air
To dissolve into the smoke of oblivion,
To arrive submissively onto the straw,
Ruminating on ending life —

To be like a bird that flutters its wings,
The brow of a storm, the eyes of lightning,
But to know that waiting for you in the depth
Is a tranquil spot —

No! To dart blindly without roads
In the abyss of a prophetic flapping,
And not to pity myself, a crushed bug,
If only I could!

1923

***

I will never forget you
Young boy at the Fastiv Train Station!
Let poets cover the path
With snowfall of azealeas,
From gilded goblets let them drink
A liquer steeped in ideals,
I remember your gaunt chest
And sunken eyes.

I remember: your eyes were
Two hungry, black embers,
The trains whistled and hummed
The black marketeers were laughing raucously.
You said to me... Mother left...
She'll be back... In two minutes...
Tiny gray creatures were crawling
Along your face.

1923

***

For the entire day shacked in cauldrons
The stiflingly heavy asphalt boils,
And white dust, prickly and thick,
Falls on your lungs like poison.

A forgotten girl is walking along
The hot cobblestones — from under arrow-like
Lashes her clear gaze shines like a lake,
One not bound in ice.

The breathing of the city in the July heat
Is the agony of a hellish horse.
The wind brings silence from afar,
The pangs of the day are dying out in the chill.

And along the pavement, as though they were pilgrims,
Stone masons are walking with bags under their eyes.

1922-1924

THE WINDOWS SPEAK

The distance of the autumn evening
Began to ring through thin ice.
I, the last who met with you,
Perhaps, am the first, earth, who understood

The uneasy voices of flocks of ducks,
The whistle of wings in drunken darkness…
I, mad, stood up on my knees,
I shout: drink up my soul—just drink it!

You pour grain with honey,
You plait, you bring together—you!
And above the winter you collect flocks
And ring through the ice to them: fly!

It will whistle, caw and disappear.
A branch fell onto icy moss.
Windows turn red at the forest's edge,
Eyes of dark and clear unease.

THROUGH A STORM AND SNOW (1925)

RAIN

Beneficial, long-awaited.
Covered with a wondrous sheen,
A golden guest of the evening
Fell briskly, freshly, with a ring,
Onto the ashen buildings
Of the ravenous suburbs.

Open up your burning breasts,
Mother Earth! The rain will cool,
Give life and make fertile —
And with the wheat and barley,
A stormy green wisp,
Will cheer white villages.

1925

***

In the moldy and sour everyday,
In the dust of untruth and gossip
Thoughts, you illuminate like the eyes of lightning,
The premonition of a violent storm.

The sky darkens. You can hear the distant footstep
Of heavy thunder in the dangling silence,
And suddenly on your chest, clenched in hope,
A frothy stream gushes into the earth.

And the earth, trembling from happiness,
Joyfully drinks the fresh, silver droplets,
And a grassy lily bends in exhaustion.

So you, apprehensive, summon a person
From the everyday, from stagnancy, from death
To the snowy expanses of the highlands.

***

Autumn began to smell of withered tobacco,
And of apples, and of gossamer mist,
And fresh asters flicker beyond the open window
Above the pinkish sand.

In the grass a cricket like a tiny gnome
Plays on a fiddle. And what good is spring for us,
When we become quiet and mature
And wisdom covers our head in silver?

Take your traveling sack and leave your home,
And drink the cold silent depth
At the forest's edge, where honey-colored melons ripen.

Learn purity and simplicity
And, treading on a golden carpet,
Forget the towers of dark arrogance.

***

Again the same Sphinx, waiting again for riddles
Iron serpents crawl along the steppe.
A descendant of the sharp-witted Daedalus
Soars like a bird of prey with a thousand eyes.

You walk, man. Torches glow,
But the haze is even blacker from them...
Hasn't the blind wandering of the Fates doomed you,
Oedipus of the new age?

***

You walked on a bridge
Above dark water. Snow soared and melted.
Feeble willows swayed like Spring.
Wind played its empty horn.

Eyes shone like burning candles.
Breasts carried inhuman thirst,
And the tracks were so childlike
On the dirty gray snow.

A poor stray strand of hair protruded,
A white scarf wept in the haze —
And it seems: a snowflake is melting,
Dying on the ground.

***

Winter lay down. Covering the roads.
Houses shiver from the cold. Threshing barns
Conceal the meager and wretched rye,
The frost paints threats on the window.

Whoever goes alone, in silence, aimlessly
Through the blue snowdrifts is miserable.
Only in a group can you cross with a roar
With songs through dense forests and wastelands.

And at the time when white peacocks shed feathers
Onto the silence of villages onto gaunt gardens.
I step out into the snow-covered yard —
And immediately become young and joyful.

For along the road with meager beggar's sacks
And with the power of thought, will, and arms
Infallibly, inconquerable, young lads
Advance straight into the far-off distance.

Once the truths of Pythagoras were sought,
And the fire of science burned for high priests.
But now a peasant dressed in a homespun overcoat
Plows the world's fallow fields.

***

This new age Mykula[16] will give the earth
Unknown strength — and the earth will bloom,
And the field will become like a gold-belted waist,
And plowed fields will tenderly bring up new spouts
                                        of winter crops.

And they walk and walk. And on the threshhold a mother
Waved her tear-stained sleeve...
And large-flaked, shaggy snow fell
Peacefully and majestically over the village.

1925

---

16   The legendary folkloric tillerman superhero (bohatyr) known for his enormous strength.

WHERE ROADS MEET (1929)

***

Some build temples for the gods,
Halls for the rich, and decorate in the high relief
Of bright pediments or in the lines of columns,
Satisfying refined but limited taste —

But, beneath the beech trees where roads cross,
Taking joyful simplicity as my law,
I have hewn out a small house, and, like a lasting dream,
My measuredly modest life flows.

And I never begrudge my guests:
Whatever grows on this nurtured soil
Is planted in the spring and watered with my toil.

There are goats in the pen, so believe me then:
Nowhere is tastier cheese aged,
And you can't buy a friendly word for money!

February 26, 1928

HUMANITY

For Pavlo Tychyna[17]

Like a round, red-sided apple
The day rolled ripe and heavy,
And the night with a slow wave of a hand
Writes wide shadows with black coal:

With a sweet arrow a late bloom,
Stealing up, the wounds the frost.
The earth resounds like a shoed hoof.
Winter will come — and will not deceive the heart.

Everything will be the way it is written in books:
Starry snow, light frost on branches,
And lonely voices in the fields.

And along the snow, the snowstorms,
As though in resonant, boundless seas,
The erring boat of an unerring human will set off.

---

[17] (1891-1967). The famous Ukrainian poet and contemporary of Rylsky.

THE POPLAR

For M. Zerov

From beneath the sky warm and faithful as a friend,
It was moved beneath our patchy sky,
Like the word of a traitor. And the shadow
Of the black treetop falls onto a beclouded meadow.

The aspen trees turn silver and ripple in currents all around,
The pond oaks run like a pack of lions —
The tallest is already falling. It tears off into the blue — and dies,
Like a star at night that rises and expires.

Unfortunate tree, Shevchenko's love!
What is glory to a sick man, what are songs to a poor man,
And what is a crimson shroud to a dead man!

Alone, you stand in a foreign height
And, indifferent for an entire century to a foreign language,
You remain silent, counting your last days.

Chernihiv. Summer 1926.

THE KISS

I caught up with her in a dark thicket.
Already lying among the fragrant grasses,
She fended me off with her springy arms.
She finally grew quiet — and a wondrous wonder happened:
Her lips cursed me and all my kin,
Like a crimson flower, she stretched out her goblet
To me, filled with sweet exhaustion.
Her strong and shapely legs tired from runnng
Looked like white marble under the mute moon,
And in a quiet voice, raspy and wondrous,
She shouted out: "Merciless conqueror!
Falling in this battle was near and dearest to my heart."

1925

THE SOUND
AND ECHO
(1929)

***

Flocks run, horses neigh, a heavy bull
Snorts in the lush pasture —
Prophetic black birds flashed,
And a black shadow will capture all that lives.

How joyfully the singing storm tears apart
And whips a frightened campfire,
How the rain slashes, how the drunken wind whistles,
Through the stream of which the distance floats!

Be joyful, earth! Drink the dreadful libations,
Accept a kiss like the strike of a sword,
Fall into the iron embraces of joy!

Already a new life looks out
From behind your back — and the voice of a nightingale
Through the thunder and roar rolls and gushes forth.

DROUGHT

1

She walks through the fields pale and bony.
Gray dust covers her clothing,
She has a dull scythe in her gaunt hands.

2

The grain turns yellow, wilting on the hillsides,
Cracked like the hands of a beggar,
And the valleys sleep in restlessly infirm dreams —

3

The loud and ringing song of joyful harvest time
Does not echo along the dew:
Just weeds, thorns of the thistle,

4

The wretched tillerman will meet in the field
The deathly pallor of lifeless stalks.
Once again there is a mismatched duel with hunger,

5

Again the black jackdaws of mourning cover
A land where the wheat should be golden,
Where all life, like a luxurious water lily, would bloom.

6

Do you await a miracle? Do you go to the choir loft to sing,
My brother? Do you go to a monastery
Where our ancestors, now covered in moss, once used to pray?

7

It is in vain that you raise your gaze:
The sky is silent, red-hot and empty, and a
Hundred-headed beast rises from the bowels of the earth.

8

Devout prayers will not save you,
Nor church candles that melt fiery wax,
Nor futile tears or anxious shrieks!

9

I look at you all, at the ant-like flurry of people
With names like Petro, Hrystsko, Palazhka, Marichka —
And a thought burns the heart as though it were a glowing coal.

10

And who is it scratching helter-skelter
The way they used to scratch in the stone age,
Who is it beckoning wizards and sorceresses?

11

Or with a needless rebuke and petty reproach
Scatter a dream through which centuries have slept?
Oh, if only there were words like long-awaited thunder
That would tear the curtain of the heavens in half!

THE BEGINNING OF A LEGEND

It was evening. The stars quietly came alive
Like roses in a pale-blue glass,
And unnoticeably to my eyes,
The caressing, warm lines of the earth disappeared.

Large and small sails began to flutter
In the sea. Birds flew past
In a semi-transparent and soft haze,
When life can't be seen but dreamt —

And everything disappeared. All borders and boundaries
Melted away. And then a lad said
To his girl: the sea no longer conceals its secrets —
We are one with it. Now neither fear

Nor hunger will stop us. We'll float onward
This way as long as the oars
Serve us. We don't need
A goal or signs. Just for the wave to carry us...

PUBLISHED OUTSIDE
OF COLLECTIONS

***

The city shines in lights,
People, stone and noise…
I am swimming though seas
Of quiet, despairing thoughts.

The city lights shine,
A din, people bustling…
Who is the dreaded one sharpening
The scythe of time above us?

1911

A VILLAGE SONNET
(From winter recollections about summer)

The wide green field is billowing,
Cornflowers shine like tiny blue stars,
On the thin stalks cool droplets
Of the rain that has passed joyfully glimmer.

And a girl, dotted with flowers,
Walks the way a swan floats on water,
And her bright young eyes, like flowers,
Play in radiant lights.

They shine to me so invitingly
That golden strings quietly quiver in my heart,
And once again my songs float and echo.

There in the meadow — birds chatter on,
And I feel happy in my soul, and quiet peace…
The wide green field is billowing.

1912

THE FLYING BOAT
*The Second Part of the Lyric Poem
"On White Islands"*

I

I'll make myself a boat of dreams
And oars of songs,
I'll fly up where the bright
Day quivers and shines,

> I'll fly up,
> Forsake the earth.
> Forsake the mire!
> I'll spiral in the sky,
> Quaffing it,
> The sky — wine...

Isn't this azure wine
That smells of spring?
And the clouds are golden foam
Of translucent wine.

> I fly up,
> Forsake the earth,
> Forsake all humankind...
> I sing a song
> And forget
> The misery and the dirt.

II

I launch the boat I made of dreams
> To the clouds — to the white islands,

Beneath my tiny oar the supple wind swirls,
> My brother above all brothers.

I launch the boats — hey! Fly like an arrow
> With chest puffed out like a swan, slice the azure.

Gaze — ha!.. There below — the kingdom of evil
> Lies in a gray haze.

III

Again I am on the white islands,
On tranquil, dreamwafting
> Clouds.

I've forgotten sorrow, lament and fear,
I quaff pure
> Beauty...

IV

Cranes!..
From a far-off land in a long line
With tender cries they fly up
All the way beneath the cloud so they become a cradle
For my dreams and me.

In the silent haze
The wedge of cranes melts and hides,
Its song dies out in the distance...
The island-cradle quietly sways,
Swan-fairies bring dreams to me...

V

You're comical for me, white cloud!
I want to go higher! I'm floating!

O, my boat! Look: the stars there —
Float off that way! Fly there!

What are former enchantments to me —
I'm living the desires of new ones...
Fly off, float into the wide expanses!
"Cloud, don't wait for me any longer!"

VI

A falcon spirals at my height,
And says something to me...
My falcon friend! Let's fly up,
Let's blaze with youthful fire!

The falcon flies with me toward the destination,
The falcon, the wind, and I are brothers...
The falcon... so strange!.. has descended.
Ah, he's left his children behind!

VII

Once again it's just the two of us with the wind...
And the wind has tired,
Lowering its wide wings,
Falling to the ground.

It will doze there
On the azure horizon,
Or on a green field
Will quietly spread out its wings.

And I – continue rushing forward,
My boat has not broken,

My joy is powerful,
And my arms have not grown weary.

VIII

The earth has already covered the sun,
In black darkness I fly toward the stars,
And I sing of freedom, pride and
    Space.

A comet with a golden tail
Scatters translucent sparks...
Below is the earth — dumb and blind.
    Sleeping like a rock.

What beauty! O gaze — earth!
What is it... you can't see.
You're sleeping in the embrace of vanity
    And impure desires...

IX

Still far off is a myriad of the bright stars, desired stars...
I take a deep breath and fly up into the distance...
Until the boat breaks and eyes see this expanse.
Stay away fatigue and sadness!
Stay away base thoughts and thoughts of the past,
Glory, clear and sacred distance!
I am free now, like a song, and freer than the birds...
Stars... freedom... solitude!..

1914

TO MYKOLA ZEROV

In love with the beauty of words,
With the solitary foam of all the Venuses,
You magically understood
The bronze Romans as well as Tychyna.

Forgive me for writing you with familiarity,
Like a son of the groves and of tradition.
In days of battling and the daily bustle
You're a patrician sent by God.

December 23, 1922

***

Monotonous days pass,
Ones that scrape, like a heavy yoke;
And we in June, as we did in May,
Are waiting for miracles that don't appear.

In vain our sleepless chief
Has evened our ballast with the boat.
There is the distance, there the blue, there a salty wave.
There are the scents of unknown grass.

There golden dolphins play,
Catching up to the stern.
Their raylike splashes of foam are
Strong, like fragrant wine.

But here the wall is solid and hard-hearted
And a black outline of mute gratings.
And like a lazy cart driver
The change of boring days shakes.

The postman dozes in dust,
Hundreds of sleepy bugs circle,
And the poor heart forgets
About joy, toil and movement.

You don't know where the station will be,
You can't guess which way the road leads.
It's useless to look and ask:
Everything is silent and everyone.

A monotonic bell sings,
Nothing looms anywhere,
And just the sleepless village chief
Hails once in a while: who's that sleeping?

Hasn't that, which we dreamt in spring
Passed forever?
Stop, wake up, cart driver!
Dear, the walls are silent!

1929

PROMETHEUS

Prometheus, Prometheus!
Your predatory vulture has flown away,
It did not drink up your living blood,
It did not pick at your living flesh.

Rusty shackles have broken apart,
The rock has disintegrated into dust,
The titan has the triumphant Caucausus
Beneath his foot.

Wind moves, the sun shines,
Cranes fly at midnight,
Like the shouts of cranes
Human voices ring.

Prometheus, Prometheus!
The black vulture does not cling:
Your unquenchable fire
Has forever chased him away.

1932

MEDITATION

The evening sneaks up slowly into my poor heart,
It's quiet there, and I feel for the world, as well as for the day,
It's as if I passed through in futility, singing,
                             over mountains and valleys,
Across cheerful meadows, along abysses dark as clouds.

My friend, I still don't know your face or name,
Young wayfarer who's just now begun his path!
Know — that I came to understand this late! —
                             that every moment is a seed
From which flowers and lethal herbs grow.

Give love and attention to the good sprouts,
Pitilessly root out the evil and poisonous weeds,
Love the pure water that satisfies parching thirst,
And hearts that avoid the road of affrontery and deceit.

Each cloud and blade of grass reflected in your sight
Are given to you only once, the second time
                             they'll be different!
We'll not retrieve the sounds, lines and colors for all time,
And never think that you'll come across many of them!

I feel for everything that drifts near and around me,
For everyone who loved me and whom I loved.
Know that the hardest thing in the world —
                             is to carry an icy heart!
Better that it be frenetic, wrapped in tenderness and anger!

I glanced back — I could barely see the footpath in the fog,
And I listen — voices barely screaming...

Dear son! When I abandon this evanescent earth,
Take my unfinished tune, and carry it off like a song!

August 11, 1944
Irpin

A BEAM OF LIGHT

It happens this way: the night's still dark outside,
While the sun rocks the earth like a baby,
The sky grows mute and the earth silent,
The stars can't be seen in opaque silence —

And suddenly you awaken. Bold thoughts
Come in a swarm from God-knows-where,
Hands thirst for work, and from the distance
The rustle of branches flows over the black poplar...

What happened? Who roused your heart?
Why do you believe that a triumphal wave
Of unexpected marvels at any moment will draw near?

It's the first ray of light glancing into the window,
The sparkling sorrow of the dawn catching fire
Like the wine of vivifying youth...

1963

THE SCARLET EVENING BURNS LOW

The scarlet evening burns low,
And ashes fall onto the city,
Above the River Dnipro
A necklace of lanterns plays.
In the drone of daytime voices
The heart is silent, sad and pure.

Night, a lamp, reflection, solitude,
The snows of still mute paper,
The soundless anxiety of creation,
Lips closed in silence,
A barely outlined task
Again lures the heart to the road.

December 6, 1963-January 1964

THIRST
(1942)

THIRST[18]

A poem-vision

> *To the 25th anniversary of Soviet rule in our glorious Ukraine — I dedicate*

You — from that tender morning
To the final mortal days —
Not like a child, not like a lover
And not even like a mother — no!

You, like the wind in captivity,
You, like the sun in a grave,
Like personal happiness and pain,
Like one's own youth and sorrow.

Like heart palpitations when parting,
Like the weariness of aching legs
That after lengthy exile
Kneel down on a father's door-step,

Like the word of a sickly child,
Like the bluish tint of a distant goal
Like a shadow you cannot catch,

---

18   The title *zhaha*, translated here as "thirst," has a variety of meanings that cannot be conveyed by a single word in English. Besides the primary semantic meaning of thirst or thirstiness, the word can signify yearning, longing, eagerness, intense desire, etc. Ryslsky has in mind both a physical as well as a spiritual thirst for himself and his nation, along with a burning desire to find a solution to the horrors of World War II and to give his people a sense of spiritual hope.

And from which you cannot escape.

Like a spark in a pitch dark night,
Like the fluttering of happiness in spring,
Like the joyful tears of women
In good-tiding silence —

I carry you in my dark breast
And in a vigilant brain,
My most beautiful of earthly thoughts,
My thirst and fervent love!

A tender sky, iron thunder,
You were, will be, and now are!
For you, for you, my homeland
Voices ring in my heart.

THE FIRST VOICE

To the great and pure water
That enlivens, freshens and gives us drink,
That cools the thirst of labor
And calms heated battles,

That in languor casts dreams,
That awakens youth to action —
Let my purest thoughts be
An honorable sacrifice.

He who knows unquenchable thirst
Knows the measure of my words.

July heat bakes the solid earth
From the swelter.

And every stalk implores
And every blade of grass laments —
Oh! The wing of a dark cloud
Brings us the highest happiness.

Moisture, moisture! — in the fire
Withered oak groves whisper,
And thunder rolls in the distance,
So long awaited-sudden.

"Moisture! Life for at least a moment!" —
In dry feather-grass it fades away…
And suddenly torn out, it howls,
Foretells, enchants and sings.

And again the return of spring,
And horses neigh above the *chornozem*,[19]
And the world, like a washed child,
Laughs in a mother's bosom.

Who knows the stones, terrain and dust
Of harsh campaigns,
The weariness of bloodied legs,
The heat of endless roads,

The fire of powdered wounds,
Gasping stuck in the throat,

---

19   The rich black earth for which Ukraine is renowned.

And the sky, like a dried-up wooden jug,
And the earth, decayed to the edge,

Who tirelessly walked forward
And crawled as an unseen shadow,
Who knows the intoxicating like mead
Blue quivering of a mirage—

He knows what a river means,
Bounded by green herbs,
Water that arose in the earth
And breathes a chilly peace.

O water! O earthly happiness!
O joy — to satisfy thirst!
Fall, having watered me,
Onto the rye, the flowers and branches!

O rivers, you are my sisters!
Circling along with the Earth,
Make her fertile with happiness —
And become my song!

THE SECOND VOICE

"Don't throw away bread, for it's sacred!"
      In tender sternness,
It happened, says the old man
      To the curly-haired toddlers.

"Don't play with bread, for it's a sin!"
      Still talking to the infant,

Restraining happy laughter,
> It happened, says mother.

The children grew, from infants
> They were made into grown-ups,
And what was heard
> Ten years ago is forgotten later,
And with good reason we entered
> The word "sin" into the archive,
Having begun curly-haired childhood
> With the new words.

Nevertheless there remains for us
> (And this is not an oversight)
A deep veneration always —
> Yes! — for the s a c r e d bread!

For labor is beautiful, though sweat is abundant,
> For the honey spirit of rye
Carries life to the people of the world
> And gives birth to human tongues.

He who sows a golden kernel
> Into the fiery strength of the earth
Himself will grow as wheat
> On the field common to mankind.

THE THIRD VOICE

The arm of omniscient spring
Sways the dampened birdcherry bushes,

And the heart challenges
The nightingale's song to a duel.

In every fragrant bunch,
In every flower that sprouts,
My life, my song and blood,
Flows as a bubbling stream.

And ursine tracks converge
To you, O passion, to your feet,
And the snow of cherry trees circles
Around the white clothing.

O dear, white, snow-winged one,
You flew down and arrived,
Unfurled your arms open wide,
And tossed silk off your brow.

As though from wonder
Pupils unfurled wide as the night,
And a dream that will not stop dreaming forever
Rolls from the green roadsides.

And fragrant flowers bow down,
Melting on dear lips.
And night in an amber necklace
Till morning stands at the doors.

> *The curtain of the past fell away.*
> *Silhouettes rise in the mist.*

FIRST SILHOUETTE

A little boy in torn garb,
A little bag: an onion and bread.
And evening and weariness and towers
Of a tall city. "Once upon a time!"

Whenever you stumble, don't fall.
Strive, enter, obtain!
Whenever you cannot at least take, then steal!
No! Take! Take away! Grab!

The sickness of the pale day
Bows down at the feet of night,
And splotches of mud. "Off the road!" —
A chubby landlord on a horse.

SECOND SILHOUETTE

She sings and sews
And no one knows
Where she finishes her pattern,
And where she starts her song.

She'd sing for the whole world,
Embroider for the whole earth!
A house. Mother's ill.
Moldy bread on the table.

"Have you grown tired, my child?
Go and borrow some wood!"

A lifeless knee[20] is bent.
The night. In the heart is eternal night.

SILHOUETTES

There are many, many, many of them.
Dark wrinkles on gaunt faces.
Some are mutilated, some are drawn stiff,
Some are murdered, all of them are tormented.

The world is a rainbow that stretches
Clear to the sky from the river to the forest,
And one can see through a rainbow curtain
The faint tracing of a fisherman and skiff.

But for them — not a fisherman or skiff,
Or a rainbow, not the sky, or forest.
There is only the wheezing of hollow conversations,
There is only the noose that crushes the throat.

There are many, many, many of them...
The pain of the back and the curse of a slave...
Cursed, damned and not quite damned enough...
And a battle rises over the earth.

---

20   *Kolino* in a biblical sense can can also mean "tribe"or "generation."

A VOICE

In a Petersburg snow-drift
On a petrified carthorse
Alexander the Third came to a halt,
Having brought the people under a yoke.

Russia naked in the frost
Warms itself with free wine,
And Nicholas embraces
A drunken peasant from Tobolsk.[21]

O, give way, eternal mountains!
This is the one in the gray homespun coat
That the infirm Petrashevets[22] saw
In a conqueror's dream.

And you, and you, my native people,
Among our strangled brothers...

---

21   A reference to Rasputin, the crazed charismatic monk who was so influential on Tsar Nicholas II, owing to the former's ability to ease the bleeding of the tsar's hemophiliac son.

22   A reference to Dostoevsky, who suffered from epilepsy and emphesema, and whose activity with the Petrashevsky Circle led to his arrest and imprisonment.

Hasn't the Bronze Horseman[23] stopped the horse
At the edge of the abyss for this?

BREATH OF THE STORM

St. Isaac's Cathedral[24] stood darkly troubled,
And the horseman failed to jump from hunger
When drunken Rasputin
Sold Russia piece by piece.

The Neva moaned with sadness,
The war shuddered in typhus,
When in the Tavrida Hall
Loud haggling went on.

Then the field and sea stirred,
In action — the word enlivened,

---

23   The famous equestrian statue of Peter the Great by Falconetti in Petersburg. The statue is the subject of Alexander Pushkin's poem "The Bronze Horseman." The image also appears in Taras Shevchenko's poem "Son" (A Dream) as well as in Adam Mickiewicz's poetry. Rylsky penned a Ukrainian translation of the Pushkin poem.

24   Gold-domed St. Isaac's Cathedral near the Neva River in Petersburg.

When from the insurgent Aurora[25]
An immortal watchword began to drone.

A free breath of melted snows,
The bitterness of riverside grasses...
The gentry's tsarist, sleepy Smolny[26]
Became the fortress of the nation.

O, enough of wounding with reproach
When a sharp sword is needed!
The right hand of Ilyich[27] has shaken
The Ksheschinsky Palace[28] like the forum.

---

25   The Russian cruiser whose crew mutineed at the start of the Russian Revolution in 1917. The first shot from the cruiser marked the start of the assault on the Tsar's Winter Palace in Petersburg.

26   A building occupied by the Soviets in which Vladimir Lenin declared the Bolsheviks had taken power from the Provisional Government of Alexander Kerensky.

27   Vladimir Ilyich Lenin. Lenin was often called by his patronymic Ilyich (i.e., the son of Ilya).

28   The palace of the former lover of Tsar Nicholas II, ballet dancer Mathilda Kshesinskaya, which was occupied by the Bolsheviks for a time. Vladimir Lenin often gave speeches from the balcony.

A FAIRY TALE

A fairy let go a golden clew,
A child followed after it to the world,
And every step opened up spaces,
And the swanlike distance fluttered.

A mother lay, ill for a long time,
And would not let go of her fair child, —
That same night she escaped through a window
In search of healing medicine for her mother.

She went through thickets and ravines,
And where the road came to a fork —
A golden thread led the child
Like a faithful friend to the water of life.

The fairy said that on the earth
A certain cold spring rings like a bell,
And faithfully on guard there stands
For her, the brave fiance of the child.

Like the moon he has a proud bearing
And bright eyes like azure stars,
From under stones in harsh fighting
He, like a spark, hewed out the spring.

The child walked and the rugged path
Often led to jungles and black thickets,
Where snakes hiss, where wicked animals roar,
Who keep a venomous smoke in their jaws.

The child walked, grew up before her eyes,
Overcame in her heart eternal fear,
And at the proper moment the fairy placed
A two-edged steel sword into the child's white hands.

The child walked not a day, not a year,
Ripened with beauty like wheat
Until she reached the age of girlhood
With the double-edged sword in her slender hand.

And many beasts tumbled in the ravine,
And many severed snakes agonized there,
Where through pine forests and mountains
The white-armed beauty passed with her sword.

And the time came. Out of a light blue chalice
The dawn, like a pearl, gamboled,
And at the edge of the abyss, at the water of life,
Ukraine met the October Revolution.

THE DREAM OR NOT A DREAM

You were a springy bow-string
Stretched to the limit as far as it could go.
You were the world's summer lightning
That illuminated meadows and oak groves.

Sadness burned in a song like a candle,
The only pleasure of bygone years.
Behind — how many walls and precipices,
Before you — like water the distance is clear.

The Dnipro River roared to green bows,
In the meadows tender grass whispered
About the Battle of Yellow Waters,[29] glory of glories,
About Svyatoslav's[30] scalplock and earring,

About the gray stone with the name of Sirko,[31]
Traced by the right hand of immortality,
About days when the foot of a worker
First trampled torn charters,

About the eternal truth of calloused hands
That built golden buildings,
About the day when self-taught Shevchenko
Informed of the lesson of anger and love,

When, like a river, early in the spring,
You poured into a new universal sea
And into the Arsenal factory's fire[32]
Gray untruths and yellowed grief —

---

29   In 1648 the forces of Hetman Bohdan Khmelnytsky defeated the Poles soundly at the battle of Yellow Waters.

30   The first Grand Prince of Kyivan Rus (ca. 942-972 A.D.) who had a Slavic name. He was known for wearing a large gold earring.

31   Ukrainian Kozak military leader Ivan Sirko (ca. 1610-1680) was the legendary author of the Zaporozhian Kozaks reply to the Turkish Sultan that was memorialized by Ilya Repin's famous painting.

32   The site of the revolutionary uprising in Kyiv in 1918.

You rose, my kin, to meet all winds
And to the question — will we be or not? —
To worlds, to suns, to brothers and enemies
You answered with the Dniprostroi.[33]

> *The mist sways and waves. In it show through the white and gold of the Monastery of the Caves' bell tower, the green of spacious hillocks, cornfields, gardens, buildings. Irpin. A young garden.*

Do you remember, my wife,
That day in spring, sweet as the pain
Of first love? I romped in the garden
With little Bohdan: we planted
Prickly acacias in the shadow
So they would give us
Shadow and shelter
For the garden. On soft beds
You planted tulip seedlings
And misshapen roots, from which
Beautiful dahlias would grow.
Friendly voices of neighbors were heard,
Bantering, shouting. A cheerful train
Carrying people was boisterous.
Each and every one drunk with spring
And a song about young Halya —
Youth itself rang in it,
A morning butterfly flew by carefree,
Like a dry leaf it suddenly landed

---

[33] The large hydroelectric station build in early Soviet times on the Dnipro River near Zaporizhia.

On an apple tree that spry Kopylenko had planted
In his role as keeper —
And again he woke us, frightened by Bohdan
Or Bulka, who in her dog's happiness
Mirthfully barked at the whole world.
A damp wind flowed above the earth,
Sail-clouds floated in the dark blue,
And the heart waited. Suddenly from the distance
I heard — or perhaps it only seemed —
A deep sound. I first shuddered
And shouted: "Geese!" It was them,
Migrating birds, the harbingers of Spring!
And we all looked with a friendly eye
At the gaggle of geese that floated on high,
And good-neighbored cries and laughter
Could be sensed in their cackling,
As here with us. Oh, geese, young geese!
Descend today to take them on your wings!

Earthly children! But no! In vain! In vain!
My garden is a wasteland, my home a prison!

> *I turn the voice to the West*
> *That smolders beyond the window.*

Barefoot shepherds
And young girls with their moist cornflowers,
Mothers who met their children at their doorstep
With a pear-shaped spoon in their good hands!
Blacksmiths and plowmen,
Scholars and singers,
Who came out of the same house
Onto the roads, wide as the world!

Inventors and gardeners
Who boldly and decisively
Cut out the chasubles of earth
To their and to our taste!
My golden-flowing Kyiv,
The pitchy Irpin[34] silence
And my rosy Romanivka!
Rivers and meadows, fields and factories,
Given life by human labor!
My bright room
With books loud as bells!
Portraits of Shevchenko and Roustavelli,[35]
A bronze bust of Pushkin,
The naive letters of beginners.
Tender graftings that I planted
With my dear mirthful friends!
The unquenchable thirst of my people
That led to steep mountain tops,
Sown with purple poppies
And encircled with imperishable laurels[36]
Who crossed out of all of this
With a bloody black stripe?
Who hurled it into the chalice of serene morning

---

34   The village of Irpin, surrounded by forests and about a half hour by commuter train from Kyiv, is the site of the retreat for members of the Ukrainian Union of Writers.

35   Shota Roustavelli (ca. 1200?), the national bard of Georgia and author of the romantic epic *The Man in the Panther's Skin*.

36   *Lavry* can also mean "monasteries."

When my son
And thousands of our sons and daughters
Saw in a fresh dream
The fairy-tale opening of the stadium —
Who threw into the clear crystal chalice
The seed of black poison?
Who cut through our sky
With the bloody knife of evil,
Who shook our land,
Damned by predatory thunder?
I hear every day, every minute, every moment,
The crackling of tender children's bones,
Broken by brutal claws,
I hear the death-hour wheeze
Of my friend and my sister,
A friend of my mother and all mothers,
Who in holy agony gave birth
To the pure joy of new generations.
I see the bloody, screaming mouths
Of the tortured and the raped,
The maimed and the crippled,
My own blood relatives!
Ukraine!
O my pain, my happiness, Ukraine!
The smoke of your conflagrations
Covers the sky of the whole world!
Ukraine,
Silver plows,
Golden scythes,
Arms bronzed by the sun!
Ukraine,
The living outrings
The hammers and axes,

Out-hums the early morning whistles!
Ukraine,
My song, my flower, Ukraine!
Who broke the windows in the snow covered school
Where they stooped over dark blue notebooks
With the crafty little heads of birds,
Blond and black-haired,
Who cared for the clean little heads
Of our children?
Who let in the wind there, and cold, and death?
Who passed on dirty wheels
As though along warm tender bodies,
Through the warm and quivering books?
How could the slow-witted victors
Not hear at that moment
That the whole world, to whole worlds beyond worlds,
From beneath the wheels curses roses
From a blacksmith's son and the son of a serf
And she who overcame the death of her word
With immortal steel?
Ukraine!
You have thundered with cursings,
You have filled with anger
To the thin golden rim —
And your life-giving thirst
Became the holy thirst of revenge!
You are alive, my Ukraine,[37]
You are alive in the great family,
In the family of nations
That the power of October unified forever

---

[37] The passages in bold were added to the 1956 edition of the poem.

**Just like the sea in its depthless womb united
Wild mountain rivers of the steppe.**

**You are alive in calloused workers' hands
That became the hands of soldiers,
You are alive, for with you in battle,
Leading the brotherhood of nations
Is that nation that gave the great Lenin
To people and to all of mankind!**
You are alive, my Ukraine,

For in the murmur of your pure waters,
For in the rustling of your native fields
For the enemy death!
**You are alive, for in immortal brotherhood
That inspires with the wind of the Party,
That illuminates with the sun of the Party,
For the enemy death!**

THE VOICE OF DAMNATION

From the deep blue sky and deep blue flowers,
From a good heart and pure thoughts,
From the field, blown softly into an early morning dream,
Like a gift, like our thrust, meet damnation!

From arms restive on their mother's womb,
From our births, from our agonies,
From song, from work, from books, from courage,
    Meet damnation!

There is no punishment weighty enough for you,
On the earth there is no leaf light enough
That would not lie on your conscience like a stone
If someone would arouse that conscience in you!

Unsated tribe, there is no judge
Who would commute your sentence of death,
There is no hand, blessed with callouses,
That would not crave to punish you for brigandage!

In the distance a contemptuous raven circles
The body that fell from vengeful hands.
Where the shout of the murderer forever grew silent,
A scornful wolf howls in horror.

The earth will not take you in sacred embrace,
Only the mighty wind blows through the world
In deserted wastelands, to waterless sands,
Scattering your cold remains.

From the field, from the sea, from the black graves,
From the black clouds of fires that darken the horizon,
From the orphans and widows, from the old and the crippled,
    Damn you forever!

> *And I see her, I see the one to whom the poets of the whole world and all the centuries brought the most revered of their gifts to suffering feet.*
> *I see a mother.*

She stretched her emaciated arms,
Combed out her fair curls,
Oh, the strands do not part —

Or has that beauty become troubled?
Or are those years not beautiful,
Or are those eyes not clear?
O, it is not beauty that is troubling —
It thunders-roars above the clouds,
Unleashes an angry downpour
Above a gray-haired mother.
Go then son, my curly-haired lad, my tender one,
Washed by three potions,
Covered in mint from the ravine,
Hoped-for, warmed!
I will close my lips — I will be silent,
I will hold a tear in my eyes,
I will take your horse myself
By the reins and lead him.

Go, go, my child,
Do not cover yourself with a bloodstain,
Your brothers stand beyond the gate.
Your brothers call to march,
To go to march, to lead the people.
I will make an oath for you,
Like the anger of my curses, I grow stronger:
Kill the enemy, don't flinch,
Straining with all your life,
Strike the foe in the heart,
For you are of courageous birth.
I will close my lips — I will be silent,
I will hold a tear in my eyes,
I will await your letters.

And the sons go, carrying their mother's
                    blessing in their breast, —
And the earth rumbles — and the waters stir —
                    and the enemy's corpse
covers the damp earth —
                    and in the heart the word echoes:

You are utterly thirst, you are utterly burning,
You are a bow, an arrow, and a bow-string,
A vision shown to the centuries,
My worldwide star!

More than once your pursed lips
Concealed black agony,
When you, a holy wanderer,
Walked along the life-giving water.

As you returned home
From the rainbow spring
On a tight yoke
Carrying two golden buckets —

A robber struck from around the corner
And broke the golden vessels.
And he crucified the immortality
Of an eternally young body on a cross.

And you, having thrown off the straps,
Watched the violent horde
Trample your children,
And the knife strikes, and the whip lashes,

As the houses and towers fall

From proud azure to dust,
As fires crawl like serpents
Along the white and blue houses,

As cherry trees blacken from fire
Herds and flocks run,
And the world drowns in pitch darkness,
And from the curses the field moans —

And your mute gaze, O mother,
Began to thunder above the earth,
Muffling all the cannons
And uniting all the sons.

And the great action began,
A threatening time came —
But there still is no sorcerer,
The quills are not yet sharp,

Still the scroll is not unfurled
To trace in purple,
How the people's regiment began to battle
With barbarians in single combat.

Having felt in their breast a common wound,[38]
And having seen a common fire,
A shepherd comes from Uzbekistan,
From Tula – a carpenter and arms-maker.

Your son walks o dear mother,

---

[38] The passages in bold were added to the 1956 edition of the poem.

**With the sons of your sister-mothers,
And on the front line cannons,
Their righteous thunder began to rumble.**

**And thought the roads are still difficult
To reach the radiant goal—
The will of victory united
All honorable minds and hearts.**

Oh, I see a figure covered with fire,
A suffering figure on a cross —
And I know that as long as the sun shines,
Truth will not fade away in life.

I believe, mother, until I die,
That a ray of light will descend on the valley
Like a golden saber —
And in a sacred hour
Into the blue crystalline silence
You will rise, my native land, from the cross!

1942 (Revised edition published in 1956)

Contents

ACKNOWLEDGMENTS 5

BETWEEN THE LYRIC AND IDEOLOGY:
THE DUALITY OF MAKSYM RYLSKY'S
POETIC WORLD. 6

TRANSLATOR'S INTRODUCTION 17

   ON WHITE ISLANDS (1910) 21

   BENEATH THE AUTUMN STARS, I (1918). . 29

   BENEATH THE AUTUMN STARS, II (1926) . 47

   THE BLUE DISTANCE (1922) 69

   THE THIRTEENTH SPRING (1926) 91

   THROUGH A STORM AND SNOW (1925) . . 99

   WHERE ROADS MEET (1929) 107

   THE SOUND AND ECHO (1929) 113

   PUBLISHED OUTSIDE OF COLLECTIONS. .119

   THIRST (1942) 135

The Grand Harmony
by Bohdan Ihor Antonych

The extraordinarily inventive Ukrainian poet and literary critic Bohdan Ihor Antonych (1909-1937), the son of a Catholic priest, died prematurely at the early age of 28 of pneumonia. Originally from the mountainous Lemko region in Poland, where a variant of Ukrainian is spoken, he was home-schooled for the first eleven years of his life because of frequent illness. He began to write poetry in Ukrainian after he moved to the Western Ukrainian city of Lviv to continue his studies at the University of Lviv.

A collection of poems on religious themes written in 1932 and 1933, *The Grand Harmony* is a subtle and supple examination of Antonych's intimately personal journey to faith, with all its revelatory verities as well as self-questioning and doubt. The collection marks the beginning of Antonych's development into one of the greatest poets of his time.

Buy it > www.glagoslav.com

Pavlo Tychyna:
The Complete Early Poetry Collections

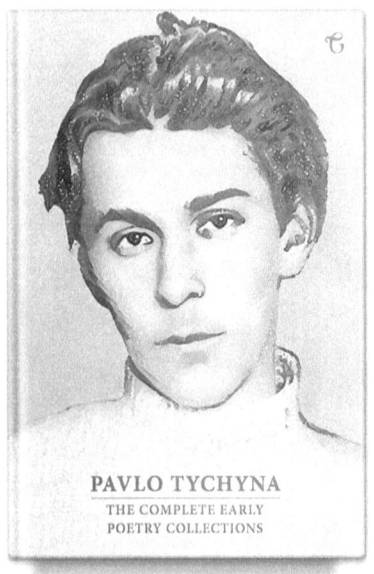

Pavlo Tychyna (1891-1967) is arguably the greatest Ukrainian poet of the twentieth century and has been described as a "tillerman's Orpheus" by Ukrainian poet and literary critic Vasyl Barka. With his innovative poetics, deep spirituality and creative word play, Tychyna deserves a place among the pantheon of his European contemporaries such as T.S. Eliot, Ezra Pound, Rainer Maria Rilke, Federico Garcia Lorca, and Osip Mandelstam. His early collections *Clarinets of the Sun* (1918), *The Plow* (1920), *Instead of Sonnets and Octaves* (1920), The Wind from Ukraine (1924), and his poetic cycle In the Orchestra of the Cosmos (1921) mark the pinnacle of his creativity and poetically document the emotional and spiritual toll of the Revolution of 1917 as well as the Civil War and its aftermath in Ukraine.

Buy it > www.glagoslav.com

Dear Reader,

Thank you for purchasing this book.

We at Glagoslav Publications are glad to welcome you, and hope that you find our books to be a source of knowledge and inspiration.

We want to show the beauty and depth of the Slavic region to everyone looking to expand their horizon and learn something new about different cultures, different people, and we believe that with this book we have managed to do just that.

Now that you've got to know us, we want to get to know you. We value communication with our readers and want to hear from you! We offer several options:

– Join our Book Club on Goodreads, Library Thing and Shelfari, and receive special offers and information about our giveaways;

– Share your opinion about our books on Amazon, Barnes & Noble, Waterstones and other bookstores;

– Join us on Facebook and Twitter for updates on our publications and news about our authors;

– Visit our site www.glagoslav.com to check out our Catalogue and subscribe to our Newsletter.

Glagoslav Publications is getting ready to release a new collection and planning some interesting surprises — stay with us to find out!

Glagoslav Publications
Office 36, 88-90 Hatton Garden
EC1N 8PN London, UK
Tel: + 44 (0) 20 32 86 99 82
Email: contact@glagoslav.com

Glagoslav Publications Catalogue

- *The Time of Women* by Elena Chizhova
- *Andrei Tarkovsky: The Collector of Dreams* by Layla Alexander-Garrett
- *Andrei Tarkovsky - A Life on the Cross* by Lyudmila Boyadzhieva
- *Sin* by Zakhar Prilepin
- *Hardly Ever Otherwise* by Maria Matios
- *Khatyn* by Ales Adamovich
- *The Lost Button* by Irene Rozdobudko
- *Christened with Crosses* by Eduard Kochergin
- *The Vital Needs of the Dead* by Igor Sakhnovsky
- *The Sarabande of Sara's Band* by Larysa Denysenko
- *A Poet and Bin Laden* by Hamid Ismailov
- *Watching The Russians (Dutch Edition)* by Maria Konyukova
- *Kobzar* by Taras Shevchenko
- *The Stone Bridge* by Alexander Terekhov
- *Moryak* by Lee Mandel
- *King Stakh's Wild Hunt* by Uladzimir Karatkevich
- *The Hawks of Peace* by Dmitry Rogozin
- *Harlequin's Costume* by Leonid Yuzefovich
- *Depeche Mode* by Serhii Zhadan
- *The Grand Slam and other stories (Dutch Edition)* by Leonid Andreev
- *METRO 2033 (Dutch Edition)* by Dmitry Glukhovsky
- *METRO 2034 (Dutch Edition)* by Dmitry Glukhovsky
- *A Russian Story* by Eugenia Kononenko
- *Herstories, An Anthology of New Ukrainian Women Prose Writers*
- *The Battle of the Sexes Russian Style* by Nadezhda Ptushkina
- *A Book Without Photographs* by Sergey Shargunov

- *Down Among The Fishes* by Natalka Babina
- *disUNITY* by Anatoly Kudryavitsky
- *Sankya* by Zakhar Prilepin
- *Wolf Messing* by Tatiana Lungin
- *Good Stalin* by Victor Erofeyev
- *Solar Plexus* by Rustam Ibragimbekov
- *Don't Call me a Victim!* by Dina Yafasova
- *Poetin (Dutch Edition)* by Chris Hutchins and Alexander Korobko
- *A History of Belarus* by Lubov Bazan
- *Children's Fashion of the Russian Empire* by Alexander Vasiliev
- *Empire of Corruption - The Russian National Pastime* by Vladimir Soloviev
- *Heroes of the 90s - People and Money. The Modern History of Russian Capitalism*
- *Fifty Highlights from the Russian Literature (Dutch Edition)* by Maarten Tengbergen
- *Bajesvolk (Dutch Edition)* by Mikhail Khodorkovsky
- *Tsarina Alexandra's Diary (Dutch Edition)*
- *Myths about Russia* by Vladimir Medinskiy
- *Boris Yeltsin - The Decade that Shook the World* by Boris Minaev
- *A Man Of Change - A study of the political life of Boris Yeltsin*
- *Sberbank - The Rebirth of Russia's Financial Giant* by Evgeny Karasyuk
- *To Get Ukraine* by Oleksandr Shyshko
- *Asystole* by Oleg Pavlov
- *Gnedich* by Maria Rybakova
- *Marina Tsvetaeva - The Essential Poetry*

- *Multiple Personalities* by Tatyana Shcherbina
- *The Investigator* by Margarita Khemlin
- *The Exile* by Zinaida Tulub
- *Leo Tolstoy – Flight from paradise* by Pavel Basinsky
- *Moscow in the 1930* by Natalia Gromova
- *Laurus (Dutch edition)* by Evgenij Vodolazkin
- *Prisoner* by Anna Nemzer
- *The Crime of Chernobyl - The Nuclear Goulag* by Wladimir Tchertkoff
- *Alpine Ballad* by Vasil Bykau
- *The Complete Correspondence of Hryhory Skovoroda*
- *The Tale of Aypi* by Ak Welsapar
- *Selected Poems* by Lydia Grigorieva
- *The Fantastic Worlds of Yuri Vynnychuk*
- *The Garden of Divine Songs and Collected Poetry of Hryhory Skovoroda*
- *Adventures in the Slavic Kitchen: A Book of Essays with Recipes*
- *Seven Signs of the Lion* by Michael M. Naydan
- *Forefathers' Eve* by Adam Mickiewicz
- *One-Two* by Igor Eliseev
- *Girls, be Good* by Bojan Babić
- *Time of the Octopus* by Anatoly Kucherena
- *Soghomon Tehlirian Memories - The Assassination of Talaat*
- *The Grand Harmony* by Bohdan Ihor Antonych

More coming soon...

www.ingramcontent.com/pod-product-compliance
Lightning Source LLC
Chambersburg PA
CBHW031113080526
44587CB00011B/960